BookLife RAPID Readers

TOTALLY EXTREME FACTS

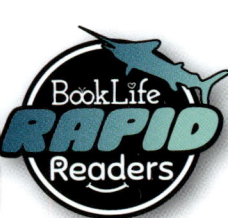

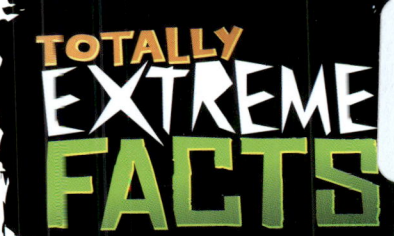

POO FACTS

All rights reserved.
Printed in India.

A catalogue record for this book is available from the British Library.

ISBN: 978-1-80505-689-8

Written by:
Noah Leatherland

Edited by:
Rebecca Phillips-Bartlett

Designed by:
Jasmine Pointer

©2024
BookLife Publishing Ltd.
King's Lynn, Norfolk
PE30 4LS, UK

All facts, statistics, web addresses and URLs in this book were verified as valid and accurate at time of writing. No responsibility for any changes to external websites or references can be accepted by either the author or publisher.

AN INTRODUCTION TO BOOKLIFE RAPID READERS...

Packed full of gripping topics and twisted tales, BookLife Rapid Readers are perfect for older children looking to propel their reading up to top speed. With three levels based on our planet's fastest animals, children will be able to find the perfect point from which to accelerate their reading journey. From the spooky to the silly, these roaring reads will turn every child at every reading level into a prolific page-turner!

CHEETAH
The fastest animals on land, cheetahs will be taking their first strides as they race to top speed.

MARLIN
The fastest animals under water, marlins will be blasting through their journey.

FALCON
The fastest animals in the air, falcons will be flying at top speed as they tear through the skies.

PHOTO CREDITS Images are courtesy of Shutterstock.com. With thanks to Getty Images, Thinkstock Photo and iStockphoto. Recurring Images – vectorplus. Cover – Sonechko57, Om Yos, baldezh, FoxGrafy, Buravleva stock, fox_workshop, stockvit, 4–5 – XOOXO, stockvit, Tartila. 6–7 – W. Scott McGill, Alex Coan, simplevect, Zhenyakot, Poozeum, CC BY-SA 4.0 <https://creativecommons.org/licenses/by-sa/4.0>, via Wikimedia Commons. 8–9 – Quarta, NotionPic, spline_x, NiRain, nikiteev_konstantin, Monory. 10–11 – Elena11, yusufdemirci, Nazarii_Neshcherenskyi, NASA, Public domain, via Wikimedia Commons. 12–13 – nevio, Magicleaf, NPavel. 14–15 – Rosa Jay, Agussetiawan99, traction, Pong Wira, Anatolir. 16–17 – J.J. Gouin, Chase D'animulls, robuart, Kamla S, Ishor gurung, Elena Istomina. 18–19 – Susan Flashman, Mandy Creighton, Picture Partners, Alan Tunnicliffe, Ondrej Prosicky, Magura. 20–21 – Karel Cerny, Sensvector, WinWin artlab, AKKHARAT JARUSILAWONG, Thampitakkul Jakkree. 22–23 – Jane Rix, koblizeek, MaryValery, chetanya kumar suman, Scharfsinn, Nsit. 24–25 – Lazy_Bear, Taphat Wangsereekul, Alfmaler, Ksenia Ragozina, Deraniad. 26–27 – Cornell University Library, Public domain, via Wikimedia Commons, Punch Magazine, Public domain, via Wikimedia Commons, Martial Red, billedfab, StockSmartStart. 28–29 – Pascale Gueret, Andrew Sutton. 30 – ShadowBird.

CONTENTS

PAGE 4	Totally Extreme Poo
PAGE 6	Prehistoric Poo
PAGE 8	Pricey Poo
PAGE 10	Poops in Space
PAGE 12	Poop Fight
PAGE 14	Poo Pretenders
PAGE 16	Poop Shooters
PAGE 18	Peculiar Poops
PAGE 20	A Sip of Poo
PAGE 22	Powered by Poo
PAGE 24	Poo Paper
PAGE 26	The Great Stink of 1858
PAGE 28	The Biggest Poopers
PAGE 30	Hold Your Nose!
PAGE 31	Glossary
PAGE 32	Index

WORDS THAT LOOK LIKE THIS ARE EXPLAINED IN THE GLOSSARY ON PAGE 31.

TOTALLY EXTREME POO

Everybody poops. However, no two poos are the same. Some poops could even be called EXTREME!

When a creature eats, their food goes through their body and comes out the other end. There are billions of animals that poop.

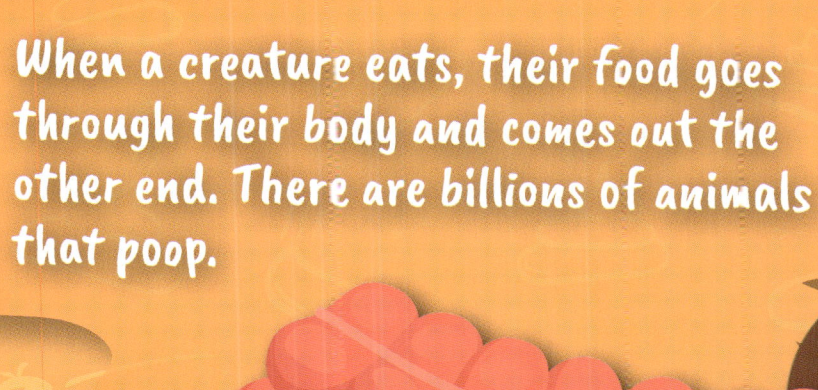

Think about all that poop, all around the world. Are you ready to dive in?

PREHISTORIC POO

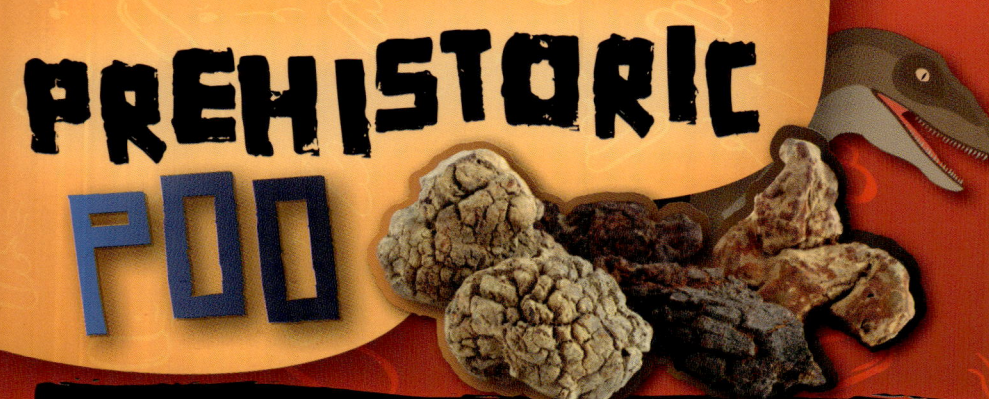

Dinosaurs were some of the first creatures to poop on Earth. Some of their poop has lasted as long as their bones.

COPROLITE

Scientists have dug up rocky blobs called coprolites. Coprolites are lumps of <u>fossilised</u> poo.

The largest coprolite that came from a carnivore is 67.5 centimetres long and 15.7 centimetres wide.

Some people cannot get enough coprolites. One man has the biggest collection in the world. He has over 1,000 pieces of fossilised poo.

PRICEY POO

How much would you pay for a lump of poo?

Ambergris is whale poop. People have paid millions for massive piles of ambergris.

Ambergris is often used in expensive perfumes. Who would want to smell like whale poo?

AMBERGRIS

Your own poo might be worth a pretty penny!

Scientists have found that human poo can contain tiny amounts of metals, such as silver and gold.

Some people have started mining for this poo gold in sewers.

POOPS IN SPACE

Astronauts still need to poop when they go to space. All that astronaut poop has to go somewhere.

There are **96** bags of astronaut waste on the Moon.

During the Apollo 10 space mission, a poo started to float around the ship.

APOLLO 10 SPACESHIP

DO NOT MAKE A WISH ON A SHOOTING POO.

Sometimes, astronaut poop falling back to Earth looks like shooting stars.

POOP FIGHT

Lots of people have used poo in wars.

LUCKILY, THAT IS JUST MUD.

In ancient times, poo was put onto the tips of arrows. Being hit by one of these stinky arrows could make someone very sick.

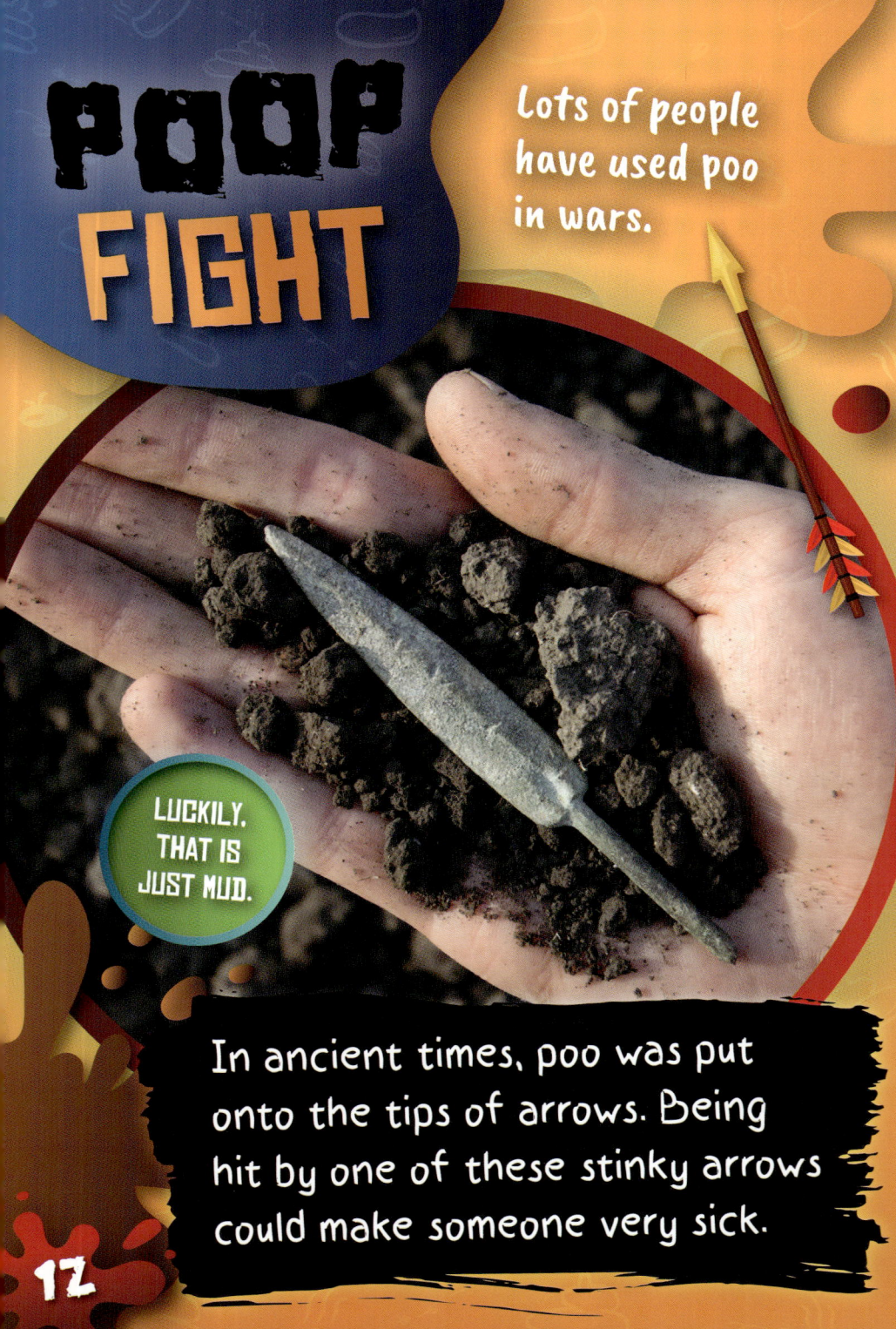

Catapults were used to fling things over castle walls. People used them to shoot poo onto the people inside!

Poo catapults sometimes made a bang rather than a splat. Some people made poo bombs that exploded into a stinky mess!

POO PRETENDERS

Some animals stay safe by looking like poop.

The bird poop frog got its name by looking like a lump of bird poo. It tucks its legs in to look like a brown and white blob of bird droppings.

Young swallowtail caterpillars look like long poops. This stops hungry birds eating them.

The bird dung spider makes itself smell like poo to help it hunt. Prey follows the smell and ends up caught in the spider's sticky webs.

POOP SHOOTERS

Some creatures are not shy about flinging their poop all over the place.

CATERPILLAR POOP

Caterpillars can shoot their poop over one metre away. For humans, that would be like shooting poop over a football field away.

Penguins shoot their poop out of their nests to keep things clean. They can shoot their poop at speeds of eight kilometres per hour.

Vultures shoot their poop... on themselves. They poop on their legs to help keep themselves cool.

PECULIAR POOPS

Some animals have very strange poops.

A wombat's poop comes out in neat, little cubes. Scientists have found that a wombat's <u>intestines</u> are a different shape to other animals'.

WOMBAT POOP

Owls cannot poop out everything they eat. They cough up <u>pellets</u> of the fur and bones of their prey.

Capybaras have two types of poop! One type is waste. The other type is soft and green and eaten by other capybaras.

A SIP OF POO

Would you drink something with poo in? How do you think it would taste?

The most expensive tea in the world might have a strange taste. It is grown using giant panda droppings.

Civet coffee is a hot drink made with poop. Civets are small animals. People feed them coffee cherries.

A CIVET

After the civets eat the cherries, they poop out lumps of coffee beans. They are used to make civet coffee.

POWERED BY POO

Scientists are always looking for new things that can be used for <u>fuel</u>. They have already started trying with poo.

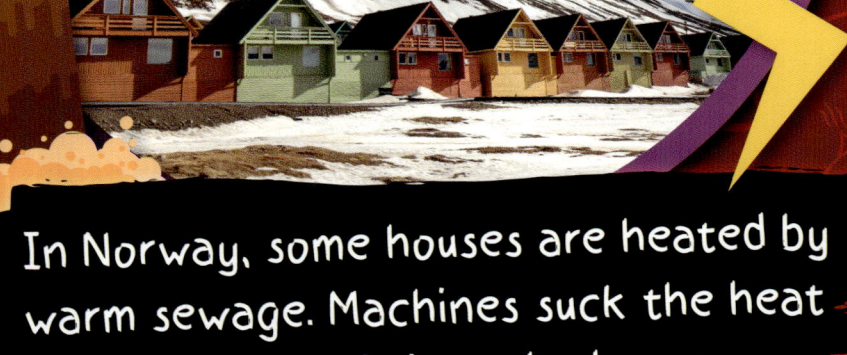

In Norway, some houses are heated by warm sewage. Machines suck the heat away and pump it into the houses.

DUNG CAKES

In India, cow droppings are used to make dung cakes. Dung cakes are not for eating. They are burnt to heat ovens.

Poo can even power cars. The gas from human waste can be used to power engines.

POO PAPER

Did you know that toilet paper was not sold until 1857?

Even then, it took until the **1930**s for toilet paper to not have splinters in. That is nearly one hundred years of prickly wipes!

Animal poo can be turned into paper, notepads and even books.

Walking into a bookshop can make some people feel like they need to poop. Scientists have looked into this for years, but they are not sure why it happens.

THE GREAT STINK OF 1858

In London, sewage used to be dumped in the River Thames. This led to a disaster in 1858.

The summer was very hot that year, which made the poo-filled river stink even worse. This was called The Great Stink!

Queen Victoria had to stop her boat trip because of the smell.

There are stories that the smell was so bad that it caused people to throw up and faint. Some people thought the bad smell could kill you.

THE BIGGEST POOPERS

Some creatures are much bigger poopers than others.

Giant pandas spend over ten hours a day eating. All that food makes a lot of poo. Giant pandas poop around 40 times a day. That is a lot of cleaning up.

Blue whales are the largest animals on Earth. So, it is not a surprise they have huge poops.

Blue whales let out **200** litres of poop at once. All that poop is very helpful for feeding other sea life.

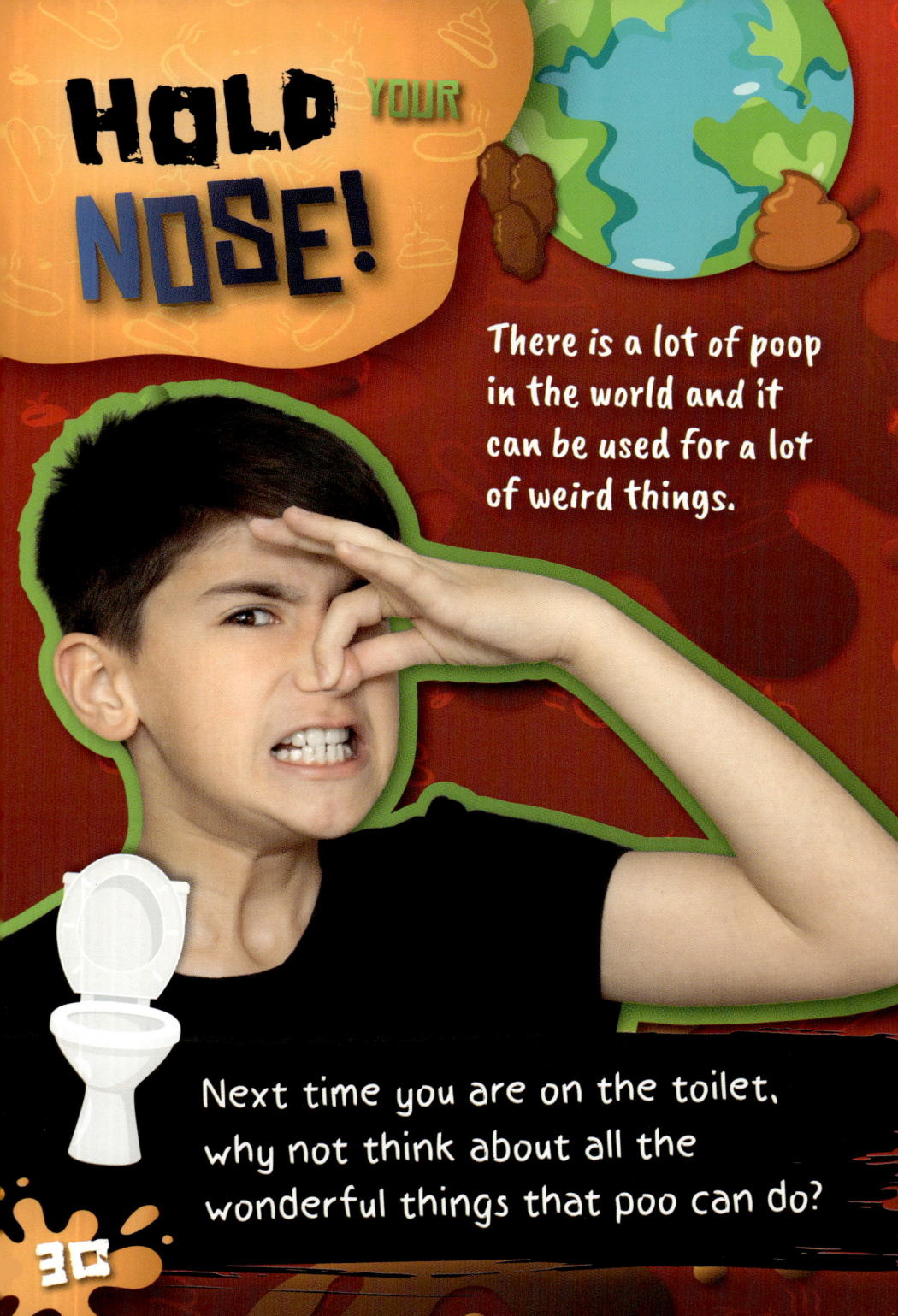

GLOSSARY

APOLLO 10	a human spaceflight mission by NASA to orbit the Moon, named after the Greek god Apollo
ASTRONAUTS	people who go to space
CARNIVORE	an animal that eats meat
EXTREME	far from normal
FOSSILISED	when part of an animal or plant becomes a fossil
FUEL	something that can be used to make energy or power something
GAS	a thing that is like air, which spreads out to fill any space available
INTESTINES	long tubes inside the body that help to break down food
PELLETS	small, round objects
PREY	animals that are hunted by other animals for food

INDEX

ASTRONAUTS 10–11

CAPYBARAS 19

CATERPILLARS 15–16

COFFEE 21

GIANT PANDAS 20, 28

PAPER 24–25

PENGUINS 17

TEA 20

WHALES 8, 29

WOMBATS 18